AVEBURY

First published 1997
© Wooden Books Ltd 1997

Published by Wooden Books Ltd.
Walkmill, Cascob, Presteigne, Powys, Wales LD8 2NT

British Library Cataloguing in Publication Data
Francis, Evelyn, 1917-
Avebury

A CIP catalogue record for this book is
available from the British Library

ISBN 0 9525862 7 4

Printed in Great Britain
by Woolnough Bookbinding Ltd,
Irthlingborough, Northants.

AVEBURY

by

Evelyn Francis

The most useful books on Avebury are "Prehistoric Avebury" by Aubrey Burl, "Avebury" by Caroline Malone and "The Avebury Cycle" by Michael Dames.

Pictures have mainly been taken from William Stukeley's book "Abury, a Temple of the British Druids", 1743, and from "Ancient Wiltshire" by Sir Richard Colt Hoare, 1819. The illustration on the dust jacket is from "Rude Stone Monuments" by James Fergusson, 1872.

Many thanks to the Local Studies Unit, Wiltshire Library, for their help with the picture research for this book and thanks to Caius Hawkins and to Tony and Kitty Ashton.

CONTENTS

INTRODUCTION

I have been visiting the great circles of Avebury since I was small and it is always with high heart and happy step that I approach the place. I have spent days there, nights there, even weeks there, and I can remember each time as clearly as the stones stand against the sky.

In this small book I have selected some of the more prominent features of the ancient sacred landscape which is Avebury - the Stones, the Hill, the Sanctuary, the Avenue, the barrows, the Longbarrow, the Dolmen and, of course, the Spring. Each of these have their own special place in the landscape. The lost valleys, witchy woods and fairy dingles I will have to leave to the fleet of foot and keen of ear.

The diagrams used in the book are mostly from William Stukely's book of 1743. I find they convey the beauty and grandeur of the place better than modern pictures. Avebury Stone Circle now has a busy tarmacadam road through its centre and constant traffic deafens visitors.

The houses in the circle now carry electric circuits. This is all a far cry from horses and hard work.

I have seen many strange things around Avebury, lights, flashes and flickers, and have no doubt that the place was built for an other people in an other time and an other kind of mind and perception, now lost to all but a few.

Avebury is a World Heritage Site; maybe one day the road and the houses will be pulled down and that will be a symbol for that time; until that day it remains a powerful symbol for this time.

I must thank my sister Sofia for her watchful eye over my writing. And many thanks to the editors at Wooden Books for their patience and sensitivity.

Wilcott, Wiltshire 1997

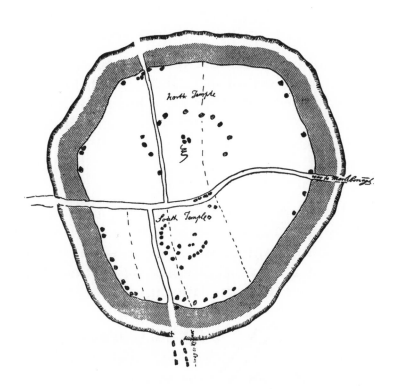

North Temple

South Temple

way to Marlborough

THE CENTRE OF THE COUNTRY

If you draw a line from the western tip of our island to the eastern point then you will discover that Avebury is near the centre of that line. The line passes through a number of ancient sacred sites - St. Michael's Mount, for instance, and the Hurlers Stone Circles. The two longest abbeys ever built on the isle, at Glastonbury and Bury St. Edmunds, lie on it.

The line marks the sun-rise for Beltane and Lammas, and the sun-set for Imbolc and Sammhain. These four days lie half-way between the Solstices and the Equinoxes, the days of extremes and balancing. If you watch the sun rise from Glastonbury Tor on May Day - it will rise over Avebury.

Avebury is also precisely at the centre of the three great watersheds of southern England. Water drains away from Avebury in every direction to the sea.

The Isle of Man is the centre of the British Isles.

Isle of Man

Hopton

Royston
Cave

Bury
St. Edmunds

Avebury

Glastonbury

The
Hurlers

Isle of Wight

St. Michael's
Mount

3

AROUND ABOUT

To the north of Avebury is the ancient settlement of Windmill Hill, where the people who built the circles are thought to have lived - over six thousand years ago.

South of Avebury lies Silbury Hill, the Swallowhead Spring and the West Kennet Longbarrow. Further away the Wansdyke crosses over the chalk Downs before the land falls away to the ancient springs at Alton Priors.

Running along the ridge to the east of the circles is the long ancient track known as the Ridgeway. This runs from Alton Priors in the south, past the Sanctuary to the Southeast and goes off to hill forts and far beyond in the direction of the May Day line. Over the Ridgeway, to the east, can be found Fyfield Down, with its great sarsen stones. This is where the stones for both Avebury and Stonehenge came from.

West of Avebury can be found two large stones, called Adam and Eve, and other barrows and long barrows.

Windmill
Hill

Avebury

Adam
& Eve

Beckhampton
Longbarrow

Silbury
Hill

Swallowhead
Spring

Wadén
Hill

West Kennet
Longbarrow

East Kennet
Longbarrow

Sanctuary

River Kennet

The Ridgeway

Fyfield
Down

Standing
Stones

5

A MIGHTY TEMPLE

Although over three hundred years old, this engraving shows most of the key places in the Avebury landscape which still can be explored today.

The Stone Circles and the Avenue remain, just, and so does Silbury Hill. The Sanctuary can be visited and the West Kennet longbarrow too. The Ridgeway can clearly be seen as a ridge.

The engraving is one half of Stukely's diagram of Avebury as a Serpent Temple. He was convinced that there was a second avenue, leaving Avebury from the west (see page 42). Nowadays people have even stranger ideas - a map of Mars, an ancient generator of subtle energies, a clue to Atlantis and so on.

Silbury Hill was first to be built, nearly five thousand years ago; then the circles, the earthworks and finally the avenue. Then they left to build Stonehenge.

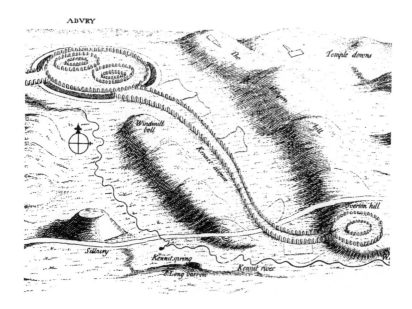

ABVRY

Temple downs

Windmill hill

Kennit stone

hill

Overton hill

Silbury

Kennit spring

S. Long barrow

Kennit river

THE SOUTH ENTRANCE

Avebury has four entrances - north, south, east and west. At these places the ditch is full and the ring mound has a gap.

The south entrance is the most spectacular today as two of the largest surviving stones mark its passage. As you approach down the Avenue, these giants of Avebury's great Outer Circle are hidden from you until the last moment.

The left-hand entrance stone, from outside the Circle, is known as the Devil's Chair. It has a place to sit in it. The gateway between the two entrance stones is very special.

In Stukely's day there were more stones than now.

9

THE SOUTH CIRCLE

There are two stone circles at Avebury inside the main outer 'Great' Circle. There is evidence that the builders of Avebury nearly built a third circle to the north of the other two but gave up and dug the ditch instead.

The south circle is much better preserved today than the north circle and you can still sense its size and majesty. A huge clump of beech trees now stands on the bank where the Avenue comes in, not even planted in Stukely's time.

There used to be more trees to sit under at Avebury but archaeologists don't like them and many were felled during Avebury's restoration.

The picture shows the south-west corner of Stukely's great map of the site. The curve of the south circle is clearly visible but the obelisk is missing from its centre.

Pasture VIII

1710

1700

Pasture IX

Pasture

Kennstone

Pasture I

Broke 1721

Kennet Avenue

Road

THE OBELISK

At the centre of the South Circle a huge stone, known as the Obelisk, used to stand. It is shown fallen in Stukely's picture. Twenty-nine stones originally surrounded the Obelisk, set at the same spacing as the outer circle - one every 36 feet. The South Circle is 340 feet across. For reference the outer circle of gigantic stones at Stonehenge, which were all brought from Avebury, count thirty in a circle.

Near to the Obelisk, whose position is nowadays given by a curious concrete marker, stands a row of small stones. These are very peculiar and serve as an excellent shield from the road should you wish to sit quietly in the middle of this most central and ancient temple.

Unlike most other ancient centres, Avebury never had a cathedral built beside it, but a nearby chapel, built out of cracked and smashed stones from the circle, offers refuge to the devout.

THE NORTH CIRCLE

The North Circle is quieter than the South Circle and only four stones remain to show its shape. I find it attracts a very different kind of person. Two huge stones, known as the Cove, define its centre. It is 320 feet across. Roads actually divide Avebury into four.

It is thought that there used to be twenty-seven stones in the North Circle, with three more making the Cove, again thirty in all. There may well have been an inner circle too, of twelve stones, 170 feet across.

The fallen stone on which the figure leans to gaze westwards is still there. It is near the east entrance to Avebury, the ancient route down from the Ridgeway. Amazing beech trees guard the way.

THE COVE

The Cove is a wonderful spot. Two huge stones stand at the centre of the northern circle. There used to be three in a cup shape, open to the north-east.

The Cove points to the spot over Hackpen Hill where the full moon rises at midwinter. The place indicated is called the northernmost moonrising.

Full moons at midwinter follow the high passage and the rising and setting places of the midsummer sun. The midsummer full moon accordingly behaves like the midwinter sun.

Not far away, east of Avebury, the two stones known as Adam and Eve still stand in a field. They are all that is left of the Beckhampton Cove.

Coves generally point to extreme moon positions.

The Cove of the Northern temple.

THE GEOMETRY OF AVEBURY

Professor Alexander Thom published this solution for the strange shape of Avebury in his book *Megalithic Sites in Britain* in 1967.

He noticed that the complex shape of the outer circle consists of seven separate curves and that four of these curves, shown here, have the same radius.

Especially interesting was his finding that three of these four centres of curvature lie in a precise 3-4-5 triangle, the 'Druids' or Pythagorean triangle.

The 'D' shaped feature in the south circle is very strange. Michael Dames, in his book *The Avebury Cycle*, says that it represents the top of a penis, reached at the end of a procession up the avenue into the circles.

For reference, this picture shows only those stones which archaeologists have actually placed. The outer circle is thought to have had 98 stones.

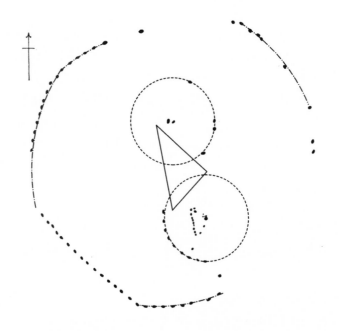

19

LINES AND CIRCLES

Few stone circles are circular but Avebury is most unusual in that it has corners! Why? The tightest corners line up with the centres of the inner circles to form two corridors. The narrow corridor points to the top of Silbury Hill.

It has been observed that if the radius of Avebury's inner circles is three, then the distance between their centres is seven. Three to seven. Avebury lies exactly three-sevenths of the way down the Earth between the pole and the equator.

A rectangle three wide and seven high gives a diagonal which is the tilt of the earth.

The angle between the wide corridor and the line connecting the two circles is one seventh of a circle, 51.4°, Avebury's latitude on Earth.

Seven is a lunar number.

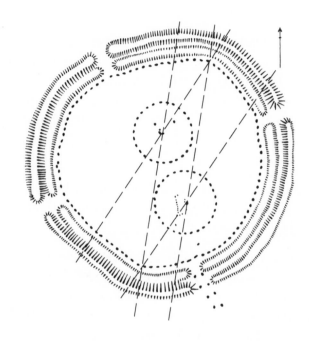

21

THE AVENUE

The Stone Avenue at Avebury is very fine. It connected the stone circles with the Sanctuary. Archaeologists believe the Avenue was built about four and a half thousand years ago - after the circles, the ditch and the bank had been finished. Then, when they had finished the Avenue, the builders replaced the hut at the Sanctuary with stone circles.

The Avebury Avenue had about one hundred pairs of facing stones. Tall, pillar-like, stones were chosen to face wider diamond-shaped ones.

The Avenue was restored, together with the stone circles, by Alexander Keiller in the late 1930's. His work remains unfinished. Stone avenues are quite rare in Great Britain but the nearest to Avebury can be found at Stanton Drew's lovely stone circles near Bristol.

STRANGE CURRENTS

In recent years some very peculiar ideas have been gaining widespread acceptance. One of these is the idea of subtle energies in the earth. Experiences vary, with some embracing an earth-dragon approach and others talking about out-of-body flight lines!

Recent research by Paul Broadhurst and Hamish Miller has shown that the straight Michael alignement (page2) consists of two currents, one male and one female. These wind across the country crossing at key places on the line. They cross three times at Avebury, on Windmill Hill, at the Sanctuary and between the main entrance stones of the Great Circle. The Michael current follows the Avenue, while the Mary winds off to Silbury Hill, Swallowhead Spring and West Kennet longbarrow.

The picture is from Guy Underwood's research.

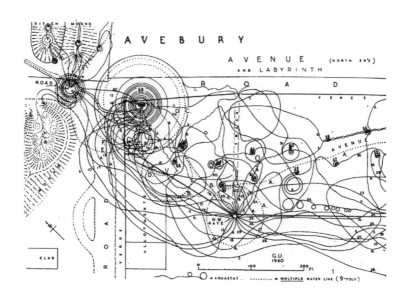

AVEBURY

AVENUE (NORTH END)
AND LABYRINTH

G.U.
1960

○ = AQUASTAT . ... = MULTIPLE WATER LINE (9-FOLD)

THE SANCTUARY

The Sanctuary today shows small posts of different constructions from different dates. A timber structure first stood here five thousand years ago, a few hundred years before even Silbury Hill was started.

Over five hundred years later, with Silbury Hill built, and Avebury and the Avenue finished, stone circles were built at the Sanctuary, either inside or replacing the hut. The stones are still visible in the engraving but were destroyed soon after.

The Sanctuary is right on the Ridgeway path.

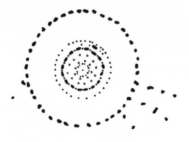

THE SERPENT'S HEAD

It has been very fashionable for some centuries now to have a theory for something one does not understand. This would be a harmless exercise were it not for the fact that people are often so desperate for certainty that the most obtuse theories are rolled out again and again.

Archaeologists are convinced that a huge hut once stood at the Sanctuary, William Stukely believed that it represented the head of a serpent, Michael Dames holds that the Sanctuary represents the Candlemas point in a fertility cycle, dowsers Hamish Miller & Paul Broadhurst find that it marks a crossing point of the male and female earth currents. They may all be right.

It has been suggested that neolithic structures were designed to stimulate, and resulted from, visual and auditory hallucinations. Perhaps, as tribal shamen say, these places really are are local interfaces between dimensions. Or was it an early Olympic Stadium ...

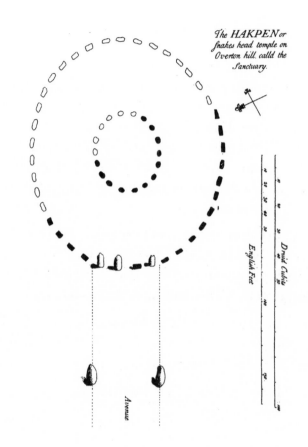

The *HAKPEN* or *snakes head temple* on *Overton hill. calld the Sanctuary.*

Druid Cubits

English Feet

Avenue

29

SILBURY HILL

South of Avebury, over Waden Hill, Silbury Hill rises from its earthy bed. It is the largest neolithic man-made mound in all of Europe. The silky grass exterior hides a stepped pyramid built of seven concentric drums. Inside are many layers of chalk, mossy soil and gravel. Hazel twigs found at Silbury's core suggest it is five thousand years old.

Halfway between midwinter and the equinoxes the sun rises over the Sanctuary from the top of Silbury Hill. Also, midsummer sunrise and sunset divide the horizon precisely into two sevenths of a circle.

People have dug into Silbury Hill and found little. Like many things neolithic this place suggests different things to different people. It is quite awe inspiring.

South of Silbury Hill is Swallowhead Spring.

STUKELEY'S GEOMETRY

Silbury Hill fascinates people - it is our own Great Pyramid, built at the same time that the Egyptians were making theirs.

In Stukely's picture, opposite, I am told that the angle of slope is 40°, one ninth of a circle. In other learned volumes the figure is given as 30°, one twelfth of a circle. Whatever the slope Silbury Hill is a steep climb and the track shown in Stukely's picture is still there.

Silbury Hill is just visible from Avebury. If you jump in the air at the stone circles, you can see the top of Silbury Hill over Waden Hill, if you lie down you can't.

St. Anne's Hill is behind Silbury Hill to the south-west. Later known as Tan Hill it became the site for a suumer fair but the last time it was held it was broken up by uncouth riot police. St. Anne was Mary's mother.

The Geometry of Silbury hill.

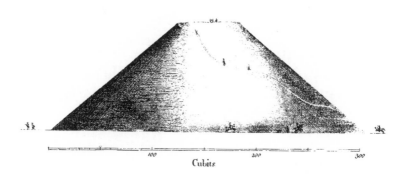

100   200   300

Cubits

33

SILBURY'S LINES

In 1969 a man named Guy Underwood, from Bradford-on-Avon, published a book called *The Pattern of the Past*. In it he suggested that ancient peoples had been sensitive to subtle currents which he could detect using dowsing rods. He proposed that stone circles, mounds and even churches were built at places where these currents converged.

In Underwood's picture opposite we see a map of the subtle lines of force at Silbury Hill. He called them 'aquastats'. In a very strange way the diagram captures something about the feeling of the place.

SILBURY HILL

0   100   200   300
Ft.

G.U.
1953

35

WEST KENNETT LONGBARROW

This is not a very good picture of the longbarrow, but it will suffice. Nowadays you can go inside and poke around in the chambers.

No-one really knows what longbarrows were built for. Some people think they were burial chambers, because bones are found inside, others think that they were early churches. Today tourists wander in and out with cameras and hippies pollute them with paraffin candles, didgery doos, and peculiar ideas.

Long barrows are almost always found on the edge of chalk deposits. They are best visited silently on frosty moonlit nights.

THE DEVIL'S DEN

The Devil's Den is still there. The farmer grows oil seed rape around it and if you visit it in May the stones are surrounded by a sea of yellow flowers and chemical pesticides. It is a very powerful place and rarely visited.

Many ancient sites were given the devil's name. This is because the devil, with his shaggy legs and goat's horns is, more often than not, just Pan, the king of the faeries. Pan, like witchery, got a very bad press for being keen on fertility and the sacredness of the Earth.

Dolmens, like this one, were often covered with an earthen mound. No-one really knows if they were burial places, meditation chambers or neolithic follies.

MYSTERIOUS MOUNDS

Round Barrows litter the ancient landscape around Avebury. There are various kinds - Bowl Barrows, Bell Barrows, Disc Barrows, Pond Barrows, Saucer Barrows, Beam Barrows and many others. Along the Ridgeway they are found clustered together in groups and boast glorious stands of beech trees.

Barrows generally have skeletons in them. Sometimes they contain a circle of stones. On rare occasions they contain buried treasure. Some people think they are representative of the stars, mapped down onto the earth; others reckon they are built where corn circles appeared or UFOs landed in the distant past.

GLIMPSES OF ANOTHER AVENUE

There may have been a second avenue leading west from Avebury - then again there may not.

William Stukely was convinced that there was a second avenue and this is his engraving of its route from his book of 1743. He shows the position of recently

removed stones with a circle. Stukely also founded the modern white-robed Druids. He was full of ideas.

Adam and Eve are the two remaining stones of Longstone Cove, a second Cove, just visible on the left side of the picture.

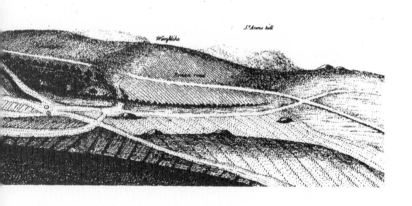

MONKTON MILBARROW

The caption to this engraving from Stukely reads as follows: "Milbarrow in Monkton. 215 f long 55 broad set round with great stones, the broad end E astnd. the narrow end W." He further writes of it:

"In Monkton, west of the town, is a large and flat long barrow, set round with stones... 'tis just 120 cubits long, 30 cubits broad in the broadest end. It stands due east and west, the broadest end eastward. Its breadth the fourth part of its length: a most magnificent sepulchre, and call'd Milbarrow."

Stukely's picture is thought to be left to right. Farmers ploughed the place up only 150 years ago, while the mid-west American Indian holocaust was going on.

45

A LOST DOLMEN

Another long-lost feature of the Avebury landscape is this dolmen. Stukely writes of it:

"In the Monkton-fields, directly north-east from Abury, is a monument of four stones, which is probably a kistvaen... These seem to be what Mr. Edward Llwyd calls Kromlechon, or bowing-stones. I believe it was a sepulchral monument, set on a barrow, tho' chiefly now plow'd up; and that the great covering stone is luxated."

Some people think these places were all covered with earth, like small chambers. The capstone is very often tilted, as shown here.

In Monkton field
by Abury.

47

WHITE HORSES

There are seven white horses carved into the chalk on hills within reach of Avebury but the oldest of all of them can be found at Uffington, on the Ridgeway path many miles away north-east of Avebury. The Uffington horse is very very old. The other distant horse is south-west of Avebury at Westbury, a recutting of a much earlier one. Avebury lies between them.

Four horses can be found arranged in a cross with Avebury at their centre. Clockwise, starting in the north, these are at Hackpen Hill, Marlborough College, Alton Barnes and Cherhill.

A final horse can be found carved at Pewsey to the south-east. If you line it up with the Alton Barnes horse it points the way to Winchester.

THE FUNCTION OF AVEBURY

Across the world people are flocking to ancient temples. Why? Perhaps it is because they *do* something to us.

Scientists and glossy media people seem to be the new clergy of our times. They tell us how to look at the world and advise us what to buy. Their latest fad is to employ sacred imagery to sell their empty wares. Meanwhile, the forests thin and the earth becomes hot and dry. This is a great pity and we all know about it.

I can only speak from personal experience. Avebury, for me, functions as a constant fountain of psychic refreshment. I believe these places were built as much for our time as for theirs by a people more clairvoyant than we can ever imagine. An open mind is best.

Maybe one day a new science will begin, and maybe then we will better understand the ancients.